IMAGES
of America

JACK LONDON
STATE HISTORIC PARK

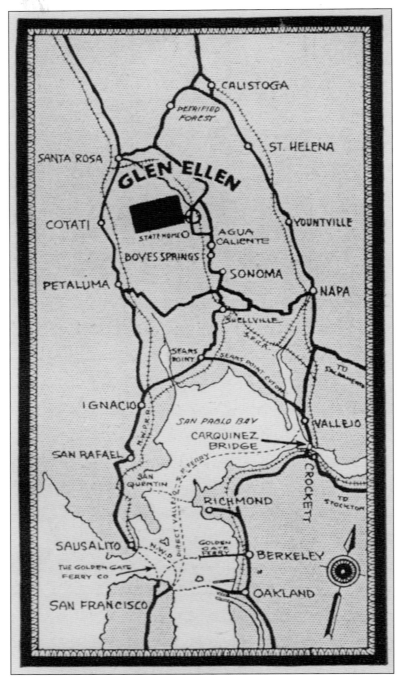

In around 1937, this map was featured in a brochure advertising Jack London Guest Ranch in the Valley of the Moon. The roads and rail lines are prominent, and note that the Golden Gate Bridge was not yet open. This brochure is also shown on page 66. (Courtesy of the Shepard family.)

ON THE COVER: Jack London, renowned author and adventurer, looks out over his land, known as Beauty Ranch, in Sonoma County, California, around 1912. (Courtesy of Huntington Library.)

IMAGES
of America

JACK LONDON
STATE HISTORIC PARK

Elisa Stancil Levine

ARCADIA
PUBLISHING

Published by Arcadia Publishing
Charleston, South Carolina

Printed in the United States of America

Library of Congress Control Number: 2014942896

For all general information, please contact Arcadia Publishing:
Telephone 843-853-2070
Fax 843-853-0044
E-mail sales@arcadiapublishing.com
For customer service and orders:
Toll-Free 1-888-313-2665

Visit us on the Internet at www.arcadiapublishing.com

Dedicated to Eliza Shepard, Irving Shepard, Milo Shepard, and Greg Hayes, through their loving and tenacious work, the legacy of Beauty Ranch lives on, offering renewal to all who visit.

CONTENTS

Acknowledgments

Lou Leal, park historian, the Shepard family, Greg Hayes, Matt Atkinson, Chuck Levine, Cathy Stancil, Deborah Large, Al Stumpf, Sue Hodson, Huntington Library, Bancroft Library, Arthur Dawson, Jim Shere, Clarice Stasz, Stewart Hume, Peter Narvaez, Brian Shepard, Steve Shaffer, Joy Shaffer, Sonoma State University Library, Glen Ellen Historical Society, Mickey Cooke, Pat Eliot, Peter Narvaez, Jim Berklund, and Sonoma Historical Society contributed greatly to the production of this volume.

The images in this volume appear courtesy of the Huntington Library (HL), the Shepard family (SF), Glen Ellen Historical Society (GEHS), Cathy Stancil (CS), Al Stumpf (AS), Deborah Large (DL), Stewart Hume (SH), Chuck Levine (CL), Greg Hayes (GH), Peter Narvaez (PN), and VMNHA archives (VMNHA) unless otherwise credited.

INTRODUCTION

Jack London State Historic Park is magnetic. It draws fans and admirers of the author from across the globe to bear witness to one of the greatest writers in history, a man who lived a meteoric life and succumbed at the age of 40. The park attracts hikers, mountain bikers, and equestrians, who can ride 23 miles of trails and connect with many miles of additional trails in the wildlife corridor overlooking the magnificent Sonoma Valley.

Jack London was a 20th-century Renaissance man. Before embarking on his career in farming, London was a factory worker, an oyster pirate, a "fish policeman," a seal hunter, a hobo, a prospector, a newspaper correspondent, a world-renowned author of short stories and books, and a lecturer.

In 1905, at the age of 29, Jack and his soon-to-be wife, Charmian, bought the 40-acre Hill Ranch in Glen Ellen, California. The land was volcanic and unforgiving, the farmers before him had little success, and the soil was thought to have been worked out. Jack London had a different vision: "At the present moment I am the owner of six bankrupt ranches, united in my possession. The six bankrupt ranches represent at least eighteen bankruptcies; that is to say, at least eighteen farmers of the old school have lost their money, broken their hearts, lost their land. The challenge to me is this: by using my head, my judgment, and all the latest knowledge in the matter of farming, can I make a success where these eighteen men failed? I have pledged myself, my manhood, my fortune, my books, and all I possess to this undertaking."

London was convinced he could rejuvenate Beauty Ranch using techniques recently discovered as well as some ancient methods, such as terracing, a practice thousands of years old. He relied on information from the University of California as well as techniques he observed in Korea while covering the Russo-Japanese War. London was in love with not only his farm but also the wild backcountry above it: "I ride over my beautiful ranch. Between my legs is a beautiful horse. The air is wine. The grapes on a score of rolling hills are red with autumn flame. Across Sonoma Mountain, wisps of sea fog are stealing. The afternoon sun smolders in the drowsy sky. I have everything to make me glad I am alive."

Jack London lived at Beauty Ranch a little more than 11 years, ultimately succumbing to uremic poisoning, likely caused by self-treating a bacterial infection he had acquired in the South Seas on the voyage of the *Snark* with mercury chloride and exacerbated by smoking, drinking, and diet. However, it can be argued that London lived and died aligned with his own vision: "I would rather be a superb meteor, every atom of me in magnificent glow, than a sleepy and permanent planet."

After London's death, his wife and "mate-woman" Charmian inherited the ranch. Working with Jack's stepsister Eliza Shepard, Charmian endeavored to fulfill Jack's dream. In 1973, eighteen years after Charmian's death in 1955, Beauty Ranch was converted into a guest ranch hosting visitors interested in riding the slopes of Sonoma Mountain and enjoying Jack London's legacy. Eventually, the Shepard family chose to focus on developing a world-class vineyard on the land that had hosted some of the first California commercial vineyards almost a century earlier. Some of the property was donated to the State of California, enabling the creation of Jack London State Historic Park in 1959. Since the original donation of 39 acres, the park has grown to 1,400 acres, almost exactly the size of London's Beauty Ranch in its heyday.

In 2011, California State Parks announced the closure of up to 70 parks—one quarter of all state parks—selecting those that were underutilized and losing money. The closure list included three Sonoma Valley parks, including Jack London State Historic Park. For years, budgetary pressures had forced the department of parks and recreation to defer maintenance in the park on many of the buildings and the lake. While the cottage, silos, and Pig Palace were restored, other stone buildings were in need of major restoration, including the House of Happy Walls, the winery ruins, and the stone barns. The Valley of the Moon Natural History Association (VMNHA), a not-for-profit organization created in 1984 to assist in the interpretation of the park for visitors, stepped up. It redefined its mission to include park operation and initiated negotiations with the State of California to manage the park. In April 2012, the state signed the first operating agreement ever, enabling VMNHA to operate the park beginning on May 1, 2012.

VMNHA hired an executive director and operations manager for the park and added new members to the board of directors, incorporating skills needed to successfully operate the park. The board attracted experts in business operations, ecology, environmental law, parks management, public relations, and marketing. They defined their mission as, "We preserve the natural and historic beauty of the Park and create innovative opportunities for recreation, education and joy. We work collaboratively with our community and volunteers to ensure a sustainable park that would make Jack London proud."

Since operations began, VMNHA, now doing business as Jack London Park Partners (JLPP), has been extraordinarily successful. Attendance is twice as high as it was during state operation, and the number of docents and volunteers has increased from just over 100 to over 400. Each quarter, the park measures guest satisfaction, and today almost 90 percent rate their park experience as excellent, the top score. Within the first two full years of operations, the park achieved financial sustainability, with revenues coming from visitation, special events, gifts, grants, and donations contributing in almost equal measure.

The special events include weddings, concerts, and Broadway Under the Stars, a theater company that has relocated to the Sonoma Valley and performs in the winery ruins across from Jack London's cottage. The location was recognized as one of the top outdoor theater venues in the country by USA Today, and the theater company has twice been recognized as the Best of Broadway for the Bay Area.

We invite you to visit Jack London State Historic Park and enjoy all it has to offer. Visit Beauty Ranch and see firsthand Jack London's cottage, where he lived and died. Visit the Pig Palace, the eucalyptus grove, and the distillery and see the barns where London kept his magnificent shire horses. The Wolf House, now a stone skeleton, still reflects London's extraordinary vision and power. The backcountry offers trails through meadows and hillside groves of madrone, manzanita, bay, oak, and redwoods, including the 2,000-year-old Grandmother Tree. Climb to the top of Sonoma Mountain or along the Ridge Trail, part of the Bay Area Ridge Trail, and enjoy spectacular views of the Valley of the Moon.

— Chuck Levine, President
Jack London Park Partners

One

Early Days in the Valley of the Moon

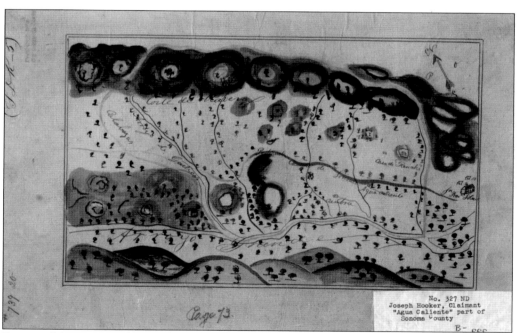

Sonoma Mountain is depicted in the in the lower right quadrant of this 1840 Spanish land grant map, which includes creeks and trees in the fertile valley of Rancho Agua Caliente. The rich land with ample water and oak woodlands attracted Europeans and Americans to an area already populated for thousands of years by Wappo and Pomo tribes. (Courtesy of University of California, Berkeley Bancroft Library.)

It is known that the Wappo people lived in dome-shaped huts and subsisted on acorns and other seed crops, game, and fish and used shells for money. The estimated 330,000 California native peoples were reduced to 15,000 statewide by the early 1900s. The Wappo man among tules shown here was photographed in early 1900. (Photograph by Edward Curtis, courtesy of Charles Deering McCormick Library of Special Collections, Northwestern University Library.)

The Pomo people, indigenous to the area around Sonoma Mountain, also used shells for currency and traded the plentiful obsidian found within trekking distance. Headmen in these tribes were more like councilmen, with special talents such as medicine or hunting. Smallpox and cholera decimated the native population, and by 1910 only 1,200 Pomo remained in California. (Photograph by Edward Curtis, courtesy of Charles Deering McCormick Library of Special Collections, Northwestern University Library.)

By 1887, farming was established in Glen Ellen. This photograph of Chauvet Winery (foreground) was taken by Carleton Watkins in 1887. Visible beyond Chauvet's stone winery building are Sonoma Mountain and the Hill Ranch, later London's Beauty Ranch. Logging and charcoal industries eroded the land, and farmers tried unsuccessfully to farm the difficult clay and volcanic soils on Sonoma Mountain. (Courtesy of University of California, Berkeley Bancroft Library.)

Clear-cutting the redwood forests in Sonoma and Mendocino Counties was a thriving industry, as shown in this late 19th-century image. Building materials were needed in Santa Rosa and San Francisco, both before and after the 1906 earthquake. Lumber, cobblestones, and bricks were products shipped from Glen Ellen from the late 1800s through 1915. (Courtesy of Sonoma County Museum.)

In addition to industry, Glen Ellen garnered a glowing reputation for recreation. Family resorts and guest ranches sprang up in the late 1800s and remained in operation through many eras, including Prohibition. Asbury, Sonoma, Graham, and Calabazas Creeks provided fishing, swimming, and camping opportunities, as shown in this 1896 photograph. Health resorts featured mineral baths and tonics from the natural hot springs present at that time. The town of Glen Ellen included a blacksmith, post office, judge, fish hatchery, mill, carriage works, brickworks, restaurants, and bars. The Native Sons of the Golden West and Odd Fellows organizations were active by the early 1900s. Dunbar School provided lessons through eighth grade, and the population grew to nearly 1,000 by 1903, when Jack London first visited the town. (Courtesy of University of California, Berkeley Bancroft Library.)

N.W. PACIFIC R.R. DEPOT GLEN ELLEN CAL.

Train travel, at its height, brought six trains into Glen Ellen each day of the weekend. In Jack London's letters and notes, visitors were encouraged to take the train from Sausalito for a weekend visit. The train station was about a 1.25 miles from the entry to London's Beauty Ranch, which he first established in 1905, on land once part of the Hill Ranch. (Courtesy of GEHS.)

In 1883, Charles and Caroline Poppe opened their dry goods store, which also sold liquor and featured local wines produced on the mountain. The post office was located in their store for many years. The building seen here burned to the ground on July 4, 1905. They rebuilt in stone, but the 1906 earthquake collapsed the second floor, which the Poppes rebuilt in wood. (Courtesy of GEHS.)

Pictured here on the right are Charles and Caroline Poppe; the person on the left is unidentified. The interior of the dry goods store shows some of the wares, including fabrics, foods, and household goods. The presence of a consistent and fair purveyor helps build community in small towns, and the Poppe family was an asset to Glen Ellen. (Courtesy of GEHS.)

By 1905, when this image was taken, Glen Ellen was a thriving metropolis. The three-story brick Chauvet Hotel (left) and the rebuilt Poppe enterprise, which until the earthquake boasted three stories, are shown. After 1906, the Poppe building was reduced to two stories. The Chauvet and Poppe buildings are in use and in wonderful repair in downtown Glen Ellen today. (Courtesy of GEHS.)

Two

JACK LONDON, ADVENTURER, WRITER, AND RANCHER

Jack London was born in San Francisco, California, on January 12, 1876. Though he lived only 40 years, London became the world's highest-paid author at the time, known for his books *The Call of the Wild*, *Martin Eden*, *John Barleycorn*, and *White Fang*. London was charismatic and outspoken, driven to excel as a writer. He died at Beauty Ranch, Glen Ellen, California, in 1916. His ranch is now Jack London State Historic Park. (Courtesy of HL.)

London was born out of wedlock to Flora Wellman, who was unable to nurse him. Jennie Prentiss was his wet nurse and raised him for two years. When this photograph was taken in 1884, London was already working. His stepfather, John London, a farmer and grocer, suffered from ill health, and the family moved numerous times. Jack's earnings helped sustain the family, which included two stepsisters, Ida and Eliza. (Courtesy of HL.)

At a young age, London learned to handle a skiff and larger sailboats and earned money as an oyster pirate, when fishing was regulated but poaching was prevalent. In 1893, when this picture was taken, London joined the crew of the *Sophia Sutherland* on a seven-month sealing voyage to Japan and the Bering Sea. Upon his return, London published a story recounting a typhoon at sea, and he vowed to earn his living from writing rather than hard labor. (Courtesy of HL.)

At the age of 19, London worked as a janitor at Oakland High School while attending classes for 18 months. He joined the debate team, learned fencing and boxing, and had work published in the student magazine, the *Aegis*. In 1896, about the time of this photograph, London joined the Socialist Party and briefly attended the University of California, Berkeley. He continued writing but had little financial success. (Courtesy of HL.)

In 1897, London, accompanied by his brother-in-law Capt. James Shepard, traveled to the Yukon during the Klondike gold rush. Shepard returned immediately, as he could not endure the mile-long ascent at Chilkoot Pass, pictured here. London, suffering from scurvy, returned to Oakland in 1898 and pawned his bicycle, typewriter, and other belongings to raise money. London's stories and novels about the Yukon eventually brought him fame and fortune. (Courtesy of HL.)

Bessie Mae Maddern, a former tutor and friend, married Jack London on April 7, 1900. This was also the day London's first book, *The Son of the Wolf*, a collection of stories about the Klondike, was published. They bicycled to Santa Cruz, California, for their honeymoon, where they posed for this photograph. On January 15, 1901, Joan London was born. (Courtesy of HL.)

In 1902, London lived in the slums of the East End of London for two months, dressing in used clothing and interviewing and photographing the impoverished conditions there. This photograph was taken by London in 1902 and depicts men in line at the Whitechapel Workhouse. The child standing alone on the cold cobblestones captures the destitution and hopelessness London writes about in *The People of the Abyss*. (Courtesy of HL.)

Peripatetic by nature, Jack London (right) spent only portions of each season in any one location. Distant assignments as a journalist estranged him from his wife and children but increased his fame and ability to earn. Here, an unidentified homeless man in London, England, stands beside Jack, who is dressed in used clothing in order to carry on his journalistic research. By this point, Jack was supporting his immediate family and his mother as well as his stepsister Ida's son Johnny. *The Call of the Wild* and two other novels were published in 1903. (Courtesy of HL.)

Pictured here in 1905 is the road to Wake Robin Lodge, in Glen Ellen, owned by editor of the *Overland Monthly* Roscoe Eames and his wife, Ninetta. Many of London's stories were published in this popular magazine. In 1903, London visited Glen Ellen around the same time *The Call of the Wild*, perhaps London's most well-known work, was published. London fell in love with Ninetta's niece Charmian Kittredge. (HL.)

Raised by her aunt Ninetta, Charmian Kittredge's adventurous spirit, open lifestyle, and exceptional typing skills made her an ideal mate for London. In fact, they called one another "Mate" all through their marriage. Charmian worked as the executive secretary for the president of Mills College prior to marriage and edited and typed all of London's correspondence and manuscripts in triplicate. (Courtesy of HL.)

London's daughters were born in rapid succession, even as his marriage was foundering. By July 1903, London was living apart from his family, and Becky (left) and Joan (right) were prohibited from visiting London's ranch by their mother, Bess. The father-child relationship was fraught with tension at times, and letters between London and his daughters demonstrate the difficulty they experienced navigating the rift. (Courtesy of HL.)

From January to June 1904, London worked for the Hearst syndicate, covering the Russo-Japanese War. Journalists were banned from the front, but London managed to make his way to the fighting. He was arrested twice and ultimately court-martialed by the Japanese. Pres. Theodore Roosevelt cabled a protest demanding London's immediate release. When his ship docked in San Francisco, London was served with divorce papers. (Courtesy of HL.)

London spent time at Wake Robin (he and Charmian are pictured there in 1905) awaiting divorce. He also bought Hill Ranch, the first of his holdings on Sonoma Mountain. By 1913, London would purchase seven parcels to create Beauty Ranch, which he also called the Ranch of Good Intentions. On November 19, 1905, Jack and Charmian were married in Chicago, Illinois, during his national lecture tour. They honeymooned in Jamaica and Cuba. (Courtesy of HL.)

Letters from London rhapsodized about the land he found: "I ride over my beautiful ranch. Between my legs is a beautiful horse. The air is wine. The grapes on a score of rolling hills are red with autumn flame. Across Sonoma Mountain wisps of sea fog are stealing. The afternoon sun smolders in the drowsy sky. I have everything to make me glad I am alive." (Courtesy of HL.)

The impressive rustic gateway to Beauty Ranch was framed by redwood logs, pictured here. By 1905, London published *A Daughter of the Snows, The Cruise of the Dazzler, The People of the Abyss, White Fang,* and many short stories and articles. *The Call of the Wild* brought London worldwide acclaim, and he lectured at Yale, Carnegie Hall, and throughout the Midwest. (Courtesy of HL.)

THE BEAUTY - RANCH

Many photo albums of life on the ranch such as the one pictured here are housed at the Huntington Library in San Marino, California. Photographs by London enhance the historical record of the ranch as well as London's travels. London's library of 15,000 volumes, in addition to letters, manuscripts, and ephemera, is contained in the London Collection, the most visited collection at the Huntington Library, providing scholars a glimpse into this fascinating time. (HL.)

Valley of the Moon"
Jack London Ranch in background.
Glen Ellen, Calif.

Sonoma Mountain is a long, broad mountain seen in the background of this postcard from about 1920. The patchwork of agriculture and clusters of homesteads and town buildings shows that for the most part, the mountain remains open land. Rough roads could be ridden by horseback or stage across the summit and down to Petaluma, but the preferred mode of travel by then was train travel. (Courtesy of GEHS.)

WE live in a beautiful part of the country, about two hours from San Francisco by two routes, the Southern Pacific and the Northwestern Pacific.

Both trains (or boats connecting with trains), leave San Francisco about 8 a. m.

The p. m. Southern Pacific train (boat) leaves San Francisco about 4 o'clock.

The p. m. Northwestern Pacific train can be connected with at 16th Street Station, Oakland, also.

If you come in the afternoon, it is more convenient for us if you take the Southern Pacific route, as it arrives here in time for our supper. We usually ask our guests to dine on the boat, if they come by the Northwestern Pacific.

Write (or telephone) in advance of your coming, because we are frequently away from home. Also, if we are at home, word from you will make it so we can have a rig at the station to meet you.

Be sure to state by what route, and by what train, you will arrive.

London was convinced he could rejuvenate Beauty Ranch using techniques recently discovered as well as some, like terracing, that were thousands of years old. He relied on information from the University of California as well as techniques he observed in Korea while covering the Russo-Japanese War. London was in love with not only his farm, but the wild backcountry above it. This card, first printed around 1910, instructs guests on travel, but it also gives a clear picture of what to expect at Beauty Ranch. (Courtesy of HL.)

OUR life here is something as follows: We rise early, and work in the forenoon. Therefore, we do not see our guests until afternoons and evenings. You may breakfast from 7 till 9, and then we all get together for dinner at 12:30. You will find this a good place to work, if you have work to do. Or, if you prefer to play, there are horses, saddles, and rigs. In the summer we have a swimming pool.

We have not yet built a house of our own, and are living in a small house adjoining our ranch. So our friends are put up in little cabins near by, to sleep.

Visitors were plentiful at Beauty Ranch—so plentiful that London printed this handy information sheet to prepare company for the experience. Entertaining at the ranch allowed London to meet his writing deadlines as well as visit with notable Americans such as Emma Goldman, Sinclair Lewis, Ambrose Bierce, and many other respected writers and artists of the early 20th century. Jack London wrote over 1,000 words a day and required visitors to entertain themselves until noon so that he could focus on his writing. After noon, he and Charmian joined guests for riding, fencing, and sometimes swimming in Sonoma Creek. His energy and humor, as well as his sense of fairness and salesmanship, are reflected in his letters, which Charmian typed in triplicate, along with his manuscripts, and filed for posterity. (Courtesy of HL.)

The first building erected under London's direction was this barn off of Hill Road, a stone and wood structure that had to be almost entirely rebuilt following the 1906 San Francisco earthquake. Buildings from Santa Rosa to San Francisco were tumbled by the tremor, and London sped to San Francisco to capture the historic event on film, writing firsthand reports and taking some of the best photographs of the catastrophe. (Courtesy of HL.)

True to his tenacious spirit, London had the barn quickly rebuilt and improved. It is shown here in 1907. In a letter in 1905, London wrote, "I am really going to throw out an anchor so big and so heavy that all hell could never get it up again. In fact, it's going to be a prodigious, ponderous sort of anchor." (Courtesy of HL.)

Developing the ranch and writing over 1,000 words per day would keep most people busy, but London always loved the sea and determined to combine writing and seafaring. He sold the idea, in serial form, to a national magazine and commissioned a boat to be built of his own design. He and Charmian (pictured here in 1907) charted the course for the *Snark's* voyage around the world. (Courtesy of HL.)

The *Snark* cost over $30,000, because after the 1906 earthquake building materials were scarce and costly. Roscoe Eames, hired as navigator, proved unable to navigate the open sea. Using books on board, Jack London taught himself navigation as they sailed from San Francisco to Hawaii. Upon arrival, they saw Honolulu newspaper headlines claiming they were lost at sea. Pictured here, the *Snark* is harbored in Samoa in 1908. (Courtesy of HL.)

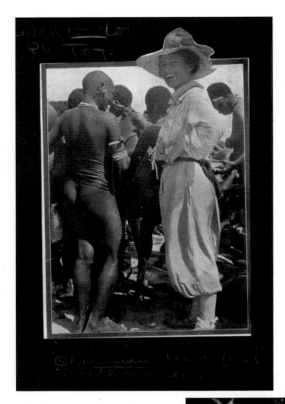

Intrepid and determined, London sailed on—perversely against the trade winds—after replacing most of the crew. Doldrums and illness slowed progress, yet they made port in the Marquesas, Tahiti, Samoa, and Fiji. Here, Solomon Island women are photographed in the company of Charmian, the first white woman they had ever seen. Melanesia, where cannibalism was still practiced, strongly contrasted with the welcoming Polynesian hospitality the crew encountered earlier. (Courtesy of HL.)

In the South Seas in 1908, Jack London and his crew were afflicted with yaws, a tropical skin infection, which he treated with liberal doses of mercury chloride, now understood to be highly toxic. As the trip continued, London's health declined, though he continued to delve deeply into island life and all it offered. This human hair costume can be viewed at the museum at the park today. (Courtesy of HL.)

In Apia, Upolu, Samoa, in May 1908, the Londons enjoyed luxury at the International Hotel for two weeks, restoring their health and enthusiasm. The day after they arrived, they visited Vailima, Robert Louis Stevenson's mountain home, continuing up the dense jungle trail to Stevenson's grave at the summit (pictured). Charmian wrote in her diary, "Driving over the roads he rode. Road of the Loving Heart." (Courtesy of HL.)

The Londons abandoned their voyage in late 1908 due to Jack's ill health. Meanwhile, farming continued at Beauty Ranch, with Ninetta Eames acting as London's business manager. His writing supported numerous households, and he continued to write despite his poor health. *Iron Heel* was published in 1908 and *Martin Eden* in 1909, around the time Jack and Charmian returned to Glen Ellen. (Courtesy of HL.)

Mrs. Eliza Shepard, Dorsez Photo.

When Jack was eight months old, his mother, Flora Wellman, married John London. Jack believed Eliza and Ida London (John London's daughters) were his elder sisters until, at age 20, he discovered his own paternity was unknown. Jack's bond with Eliza was trusting, and he knew her to be capable and ethical. Eliza Shepard is pictured here at age 20; she married at 16 and became a lawyer, working with her husband. (Courtesy of HL.)

Eliza Shepard (left foreground) inspired faith in many people. She is pictured here after the 1906 earthquake, appointed by the governor of California to coordinate relief efforts of the Red Cross, Army, and Salvation Army. Additionally, Eliza worked to secure benefits for veterans of the Civil War. Organized, diligent, and caring, she had many skills that were key to the future success of Beauty Ranch. (Courtesy of HL.)

In 1910, Jack hired Eliza London Shepard as full-time manager of Beauty Ranch. She arrived in Glen Ellen with her young son, Irving, and managed the cultivation and bookkeeping on a daily basis as well as feeding up to 50 hired hands. In 1911, she negotiated the purchase of Kohler and Frohling Winery (pictured), which included stone and clapboard buildings essential to the ranch effort. (Courtesy of HL.)

In 1910, Jack and Charmian's daughter Joy was born, but she lived only 38 hours. Around the same time, Eliza's son, Irving, was electrocuted while climbing a tree, and he spent months recovering. Letters from Eliza and Jack to the electric company request compensation for the cost of nursing Irving back to health. Irving is pictured here in the snow on Sonoma Mountain after his recovery. (Courtesy of SF.)

Often away for weeks or months, London continued his travels and communicated with Eliza via letter and telegram, sometimes listing more than 30 items to be immediately attended to. His vision and energy seemed boundless, and his expectations often did as well. The Kohler and Frohling purchase included old winery offices, bunkrooms, and a clapboard cottage (pictured), which the Londons planned to live in until their dream home was built. (Courtesy of HL.)

Named Wildwater Creek in Jack London's book *The Valley of the Moon*, Graham Creek (shown at left) is a year-round creek on Sonoma Mountain in which steelhead and freshwater shrimp were abundant in the early 1900s. London's desire to produce high-yield crops relied on water, and his notes from this time reveal his desire to capture water for irrigation. This 1906 photograph is one of many taken by London during his time at the ranch. (Courtesy of HL.)

Jack London's vigor and sense of humor were well documented. He loved to play pranks, box with anyone willing, fence, swim, dive, and carouse. Visitors to the cottage and guest rooms might be treated to a surprise such as a trick book with a firecracker inside or a midnight earthquake caused by ranch hands rocking the bed using hidden ropes affixed to the bed legs and manipulated from the cellar. (Courtesy of HL.)

Charmian is captured in a photograph as she crosses over Graham Creek. Around 1913, London wrote in a letter, "Who will reap what I have sown here in this almighty sweet land? You and I will be forgotten. Others will come and go; these too, shall pass, as you and I shall pass, and others take their places, each telling his love, as I tell you, that life is sweet." (Courtesy of HL.)

The wine industry was not profitable even before Prohibition began in 1919. Most vines at the ranch were replaced with hay or orchards. Using ideas from agricultural leaflets and texts, London sought to create a bountiful enterprise in which the best farming methods would improve the soil. London vowed to improve the rocky, volcanic-clay soil using both modern and ancient techniques. Here, workers create terraces in 1911. (Courtesy of HL.)

Research shows that London was impressed with genetics, and he sought to breed the best of the best in horses, pigs, and cattle. In 1915, the stone stallion barn (far right) and the manure pit (center) were built by Italian masons. The sherry barn, built by Chinese masons for Kohler and Frohling in 1887, is on the far left. All three buildings still stand today. Taken around 1915, this image is from London's ranch album. (Courtesy of HL.)

Eliza Shepard, shown here around 1915, worked to improve the community, helping to establish a home for unwed mothers on the other side of the valley, and distributing turkeys to the poor at holidays. She quietly arranged for gleaning from the ranch orchards and vineyard so that less-fortunate neighbors could harvest food to supplement their pantries. (Courtesy of HL.)

Eliza and Charmian were two strong women who complemented each other and allowed Jack to focus on earning money through writing and entrepreneurial endeavors. Charmian typed his work and letters in triplicate, managed his publishing records, and accompanied Jack on his many travels. An accomplished horsewoman, she was said to be the first woman to ride astride in California. (Courtesy of HL.)

Eliza and her husband, of Shepard and Company, were both lawyers who represented Civil War veterans seeking compensation for war injuries. The Yountville Veterans Home in California has a plaque commemorating Captain Shepard's work on behalf of veterans. According to Milo Shepard, Eliza's grandson, Eliza was the "and Company" of the enterprise. Eliza's life was not without some controversy; her aged husband, Captain Shepard, appeared at the ranch in May 1913 wielding a gun and claiming Jack London had stolen his wife. A scuffle ensued, and the altercation was reported far and wide. After a short court battle, Eliza obtained a divorce, and she and Irving remained at the ranch.

Jack London sailed the Sacramento River and San Francisco Bay aboard this sailboat (shown here in 1913), which he named the *Roamer*. He spent weeks exploring the deltas of Northern California in 1910 and 1912, a solace after the loss of his daughter Joy and Charmian's miscarriage in 1912. Charmian wrote of Jack's love of sailing and shares theses memories from aboard the *Roamer* in *The Book of Jack London*: "To him relaxation consisted not in cessation but in change of thought and occupation. The vessel all in order, laid against a river-bank for the night, he would sit, placidly smoking in the blue dungarees and old tam, humped comfortably on deck, his soft-shod feet hanging over the rail, line overboard for cat-fish or black bass." (Courtesy of HL.)

In 1911, Jack London began work with Albert Farr, renowned architect of San Francisco. London had strong opinions and sought a building that would be a house of "air, sunshine and laughter." In a letter to his publisher, he writes, "I am building my dream-house on my dream-ranch. My house will be standing, act of God permitting, for a thousand years." Eliza was superintendent of the building project. (Courtesy of HL.)

During London's time, these stone walls were all that remained of a large barrel room that housed wine for Kohler and Frohling. These walls still stand today, and this image, captured by London some time before 1916, is remarkably unchanged in the many decades since. Today, performances and events are staged within the ruins. (Courtesy of HL.)

Creativity and curiosity motivated London (right), and he was drawn to inventive people. Luther Burbank (center) lived nearby and was renowned for genetic experiments with plants. London collaborated with Burbank to grow spineless cactus as a cattle feed that could be dry-farmed. The man at left is unidentified. (Courtesy of HL.)

This image, taken by London in 1914, shows the full experiment. However, two issues foiled the plan. The spines returned in the second season, and the cactus grew too slowly as a result of Northern California's meager rainfall, so it was not feasible as a low-cost cattle feed. The cactus is memorialized at the park today in a small plot in the meadow. (Courtesy of HL.)

London had great help in achieving his dreams, and he also had serious challenges. By the time this iconic image was taken in 1915, London suffered from acute and chronic kidney disease. His efforts to realize his many dreams seemed inflamed with urgency; meanwhile, his monetary obligations continued to mount. (Courtesy of HL.)

Another scheme in which London invested a great deal of time and money was the eucalyptus boom. Farmers in America were eager to make use of their land, and after the 1906 earthquake, London envisioned eucalyptus as a fast-growing tree that could be used for piers, railroad ties, and construction. He planted over 80,000 trees, only to learn that the seedlings imported were of the wrong variety, unsuitable for building or making paper. (Courtesy of HL.)

Remnants of London's eucalyptus enterprise live on at Beauty Ranch, though most of the trees have been thinned or removed. Photographed by Charmian London in 1930, this tree could be seen from the cottage, and over the years Charmian referred to it as the Ghost Tree, due to the white branches. Sonoma Mountain is framed in the background. Today, hikers pass by the tree on the way to the lake and the backcountry trails. In London's time, a stage road went from the ranch over the mountain to Petaluma, about a 20-mile ride, and London was said to have ridden over to play poker from time to time. (Courtesy of HL.)

The incredible English shire stallion pictured here won grand champion at the 1912 California State Fair. Jack planned to breed champion shire horses, and Neuadd Hillside, bred in England, was purchased immediately following the 1912 fair to be the sire of London's purebred line. The magnificent stallion arrived in Glen Ellen by train soon after. Eliza Shepard developed award-winning lines of livestock during her tenure as ranch manager, and London trusted her skill in selecting cattle, horses, pigs, and goats for the ranch. Neuadd Hillside died unexpectedly in 1915, and London's valet, Nakata, in his oral history, reports London was deeply saddened by the loss. (Courtesy of HL.)

By 1912, Jack's dream home (known as Wolf House) was beginning to take shape. Solid redwood logs with the bark intact formed many of the wooden elements in the massive building. Stones quarried 30 miles away were brought by rail then by horse and wagon to the hillside site. Foreman Natal Forni was the Italian stonemason hired by Eliza, and his stonework is strong to this day. (Courtesy of HL.)

Work progressed apace on the Wolf House, which rose four stories with nine chimneys and 26 rooms. This great lodge had many areas open to the air and a library to house London's 15,000 volumes. Baths with the most modern conveniences contrasted with the rugged redwood and stone. London continued to publish works written at Beauty Ranch as well as while traveling. In 1913, *Valley of the Moon*, featuring the ranch and San Francisco, and *John Barleycorn* were published. (Courtesy of HL.)

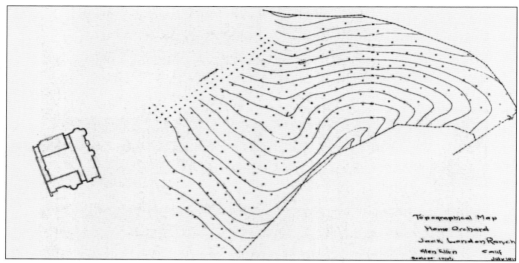

Site preparation began five years before house construction, when London's workers shaped land contours to create terraces and planted fruit trees for the family orchard. Redwoods were felled and stacked according to Farr's direction and allowed to season. Concrete foundation sufficient for a 40-story skyscraper was laid as a precaution against earthquakes. (Courtesy of HL.)

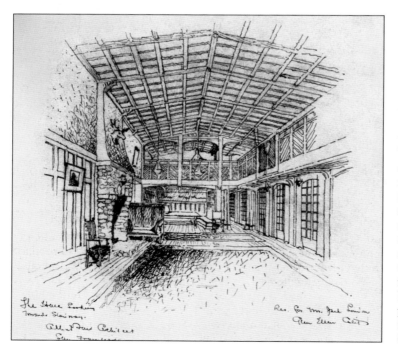

The chief feature of the house was the great living room, which rose over two stories high, with rough redwood balconies extending around the second floor. Open rafters for ceiling and gables and an immense stone fireplace lent a cheerful, homelike appearance despite the vast scale—18 feet wide and 58 feet long. Natural redwood paneling enhanced the interiors throughout. (Courtesy of HL.)

Had it survived, Wolf House would have been one of the most distinguished works of early 20th-century California architecture, a combination of Arts and Crafts style and Adirondack design. In the center was a reflecting pool, designed to reflect light into the center of the house. London planned to stock it with fish and take the occasional plunge! Readers of *The Little Lady of the Big House* will recognize many of London's innovative design ideas included in the novel, which was published after his dream home had gone up in flames. Many years earlier, London had also broadly sketched his notions of the ideal home in an essay, "The House Beautiful," and Farr and London together captured much of this idealized vision. (Courtesy of HL.)

At midnight on August 22, 1913, a fire was discovered at Wolf House, and the entire structure was soon ablaze. The beautiful redwood paneling, giant logs, and planked floors went up in smoke. The stone and concrete foundation and chimneys remained, an eerie skeleton of Jack's dream house. London's insurance only partially covered the loss. He vowed to rebuild, and numerous letters to his publishers and close friends demonstrated his intent; but the costs were great, and

the time needed to season new redwood logs prohibited much progress. A few months following the loss of the Wolf House, Jack London faced the loss of his beloved Neuadd Hillside. Both Charmian and London's valet, Nakata, noted London's deep sadness at that time, a sadness he did not show publicly. (Courtesy of HL.)

As the ranch expanded, work on many buildings continued. A blacksmith shop (pictured in 1915) was installed in the stone building, not far from the bunkhouse and offices. Edward Ranker of Glen Ellen moved his shop to the ranch and worked full-time repairing and forging tools and equipment. Edward and Minda Ranker's daughter Mildred later married Irving Shepard, Eliza Shepard's son. (Courtesy of HL.)

After the burning of Wolf House, Jack and Charmian made revisions to the small cottage and stone dining room in the heart of Beauty Ranch, adding a writing studio for Jack with windows on three sides. The stone dining room was redecorated, and here the couple entertained many guests. Visitors slept in small guest rooms in the cottage and in the old winery building nearby. (Courtesy of HL.)

In the fall of 1913, London cruised the Sacramento and San Joaquin River deltas aboard the *Roamer*. He won a copyright trial against a moving picture company and published two novels written at the cottage, *John Barleycorn* and *The Valley of the Moon*. *The Abysmal Brute* and numerous short stories and essays were published at this time as well. (Courtesy of HL.)

This image was likely taken by Jack London and shows a portion of the interior of the stone dining room outfitted with treasures from the South Seas. Tapas cloths, carved wooden bowls, and other mementos were collected on the *Snark* voyage and intended for the massive Wolf House interior. Furniture designed and built for the Wolf House is on display at the park today. (Courtesy of HL.)

In a letter written in 1914, London states, "As usual I am plugging away, head over heels with the ranch . . . I am building, constructing, and making dead soil live again. My terraces are beginning to show up and my first silo is a success." Several silos were originally planned, and the two concrete silos pictured here were the first completed west of the Mississippi. The curved concrete blocks were formed on-site, and a gasoline-powered conveyer belt was used to fill the completed silos with silage. This image is part of a ranch album from London's time, perhaps taken by Jack London himself. See page 96 for an image of the silos today. (Courtesy of HL.)

These hungry piglets are Duroc-Jersey pigs, a breed selected by London. In a 1914 letter to his editor, London asserts, "By using my head, my judgment, and all the latest knowledge in the matter of farming can I make a success where those . . . men failed? I have pledged myself, my manhood, my fortune, my books and all I possess to this undertaking." (Courtesy of HL.)

When the piggery was designed and built after the Wolf House fire, London insisted no wood be used; even the roof and doors were concrete. The circular design was an innovation allowing one worker to feed and clean the pens as well as providing each pig family separate quarters and open-air runs. The high cost of building the piggery, along with the elegant style, generated ridicule, and a San Francisco newspaper dubbed it the "Palace Hotel for Pigs." (Courtesy of HL.)

"My first big dam on the place is just finished so that on these poor, old, worked-out, eroded hillsides I shall be able to harvest two crops a year and turn one crop under; in place of the old meager crop that could be taken off only once in several years." (Courtesy of HL.)

In early 1915, a stone dam in the hills above the ranch created Jack's lake. Winter runoff and minor springs kept the lake full until late summer, when water was piped in from Graham Creek, which led to a lawsuit over water rights. London returned from a health holiday in Hawaii to testify at the trial, which was decided in his favor. Ill health continued to plague the prolific writer. (Courtesy of HL.)

While traveling, Jack sent a letter to Eliza listing 39 urgent tasks. One included constructing a bathhouse at the lake. In seven days, Eliza telegrammed him that all tasks were complete. The bathhouse had fresh water piped from the creek, a boardwalk to the water, and boat storage on each side. The novels *The Star Rover* and *The Scarlet Plague* were published in 1915. (Courtesy of HL.)

The lake is pictured here in 1916. In chapters 4 and 5, the decline of the lake is documented. For decades, visitors and those who lived on the ranch enjoyed the quiet stillness of the beautiful body of water. Over time, the lake silted in while under the management of California State Parks, beginning in 1976. The Jack London Lake Alliance was formed in 2008 to restore the lake, but permission and funding has not been obtained. (Courtesy of HL.)

As Jack's health had deteriorated, he had become short-tempered. Charmian's diaries mention this tendency in earlier years, but by 1916 he was plagued by pain and poor circulation. Charmian took solace in the horses she so loved and continued to support Jack and his writing. *The Little Lady of the Big House*, a novel set in California featuring a large ranch, was published at this time. (Courtesy of HL.)

Eliza continued to tend to ranch and legal matters, winning awards at the California State Fair in 1916 for her livestock and purchasing additional breed stock in Jack's stead. Jack's vision for the ranch had expanded, even as his health declined, and he had made plans to begin a schoolhouse, workers' store, and post office. His notes to Eliza had become less legible and more demanding as his health continued to fail. (Courtesy of HL.)

On November 22, 1916, London was found to be unresponsive as he lay in his cot on his sleeping porch. Efforts to revive him were unsuccessful, and five doctors were on hand when he died at 7:45 p.m. The death certificate states the cause of death as "uraemia following renal colic" and "chronic interstitial nephritis." London's personal doctor, Dr. Porter, as well as Dr. Sheils and two Sonoma doctors were on hand when he died. Recent medical studies have given the main cause of death to be the result of the mercury chloride applied to open sores caused by yaws for a period of five months in the Solomon Islands. The mercury would have settled on his kidneys. Jack London died at 40 years old. (Courtesy of HL.)

Years before he died, London had developed a personal attachment to a knoll on his property that held the graves of two children who had died about the time London was born. He requested Charmian lay his ashes at that location if he died before she did. The day London's ashes were brought to the ranch was a cold, dark November day. A silent ceremony was held to place the urn in a waiting hole lined with tile. Concrete was poured over the urn and two shire horses pulled a large rock (not used in the Wolf House) over the gravesite. At this time, bright sunlight broke through the dark sky to shine as a tribute on Jack London's place of rest. (Courtesy of HL.)

Three

PRESERVING LONDON'S LEGACY

Eliza continued to manage Beauty Ranch, but it was often an uphill climb. In 2008, Milo Shepard said of his grandmother, "She had curiosity in life, about physical things—what makes this run, or this turn, when she turned this to agriculture she fit in perfectly. She was a very, very honest person, not intimidated by anyone. She was an organizer, it was just natural for her." Eliza is pictured here on a snowy slope of Sonoma Mountain around 1918. (Courtesy of HL.)

Dearest Sister Eliza:—
With a heart full of love, and full of joy that you are here with us in this joy-spot of the Valley of the Moon.

your brother,
Jack London.

Glen Ellen, Calif.,
March 23, 1910.

In 1917, Eliza Shepard wrote, "Jack's ambition was to develop a model farm; one of the best all-round ranches in the state, combining a stock ranch, fruit, grain, vegetables and the like. He would have accomplished his plan had he lived, for his enthusiasm was unquenchable." Jack inscribed first editions and presented them to Eliza, his mother, Charmian, and many others. Pictured here is his inscription for *The Valley of the Moon*: "Dear Sister Eliza, With a heart full of love, and full of joy that you are here with us in this joy-spot of the Valley of the Moon, your brother, Jack London. Glen Ellen, Calif., March 23, 1910." Eliza, entrusted with the care of the ranch in perpetuity, took this duty to heart and sought to maintain the ranch in the manner Jack had intended. (Courtesy of HL.)

Charmian London focused on keeping the literary vision of Jack London alive after his death and wrote a comprehensive two-volume biography of him. She is pictured here in the cottage where she did much of the writing, beginning in 1919. Her travels, writing, and appearances were noted internationally throughout her life, and this added to the London lore. (Courtesy of HL.)

Though London had died, visitors remained prevalent at the ranch. Managing the comings and goings, the farming, harvest, and all ranch activities continued to be Eliza's focus, in addition to the added work of handling legal issues related to the estate. Charmian traveled to New York and Europe to meet with publishers and bankers, and unrest and war in Europe complicated their efforts to sustain the ranch financially. (Courtesy of HL.)

In 1911, Eliza built a shingled Arts and Crafts–style house (pictured) on a knoll above the Londons' cottage. Her home is now part of the Shepard Trust, 160 acres surrounded by what are now state park lands. After Jack's death in 1916, Charmian continued to live in the cottage they had shared until around 1934, when she moved into her new three-story stone house. (Courtesy of HL.)

Throughout the decades after London's death, Charmian (pictured here in 1935) continued to ride almost daily whenever she was at the ranch. Her notoriety and her own published works helped maintain the London allure worldwide. Charismatic, feminine, and accomplished, Charmian maintained a role as hostess and keeper of the literary flame that was key, yet income remained difficult to generate. (Courtesy of HL.)

The stone house known as the House with Happy Walls became Charmian's home in 1934. Designed by Harry Merrett, an architect married to the cook at the ranch, the house is a delightful interpretation of Arts and Crafts style, with reading nooks, a sunken fireplace, secret stairs, and fine details inspired by the Londons' travels. This house museum is open to the public today. (Courtesy of AS.)

Charmian left a handwritten note in her will: "In case of my death it is my wish that my home, "House With Happy Walls," is not to be be [sic] lived in by any one except a care taker. This building and its arrangements are peculiarly an expression of myself and its ultimate purpose is that of a museum to Jack London and myself. It can be used for the purpose of revenue." The museum is open year-round today. (Courtesy of AS.)

In the 1920s, grapes were not selling due to Prohibition, and some of the 18 acres of vines were replaced with other crops. Making ends meet was the subject of many of the letters exchanged between Eliza and Charmian as they struggled to secure payment from European printings of London's works and bootleg reprinting and translation worldwide. Income was a major concern as the decade wore on. (Courtesy of HL.)

Visitors continued to enjoy the fruits and delights of the ranch in both winter and summer. The lake, originally stocked with catfish, was restocked with bass. Swimming, fishing, riding, and relaxing were enticements to London's old crowd and to new friends who came to visit Charmian and Eliza. Relatives and acquaintances were welcome to stay, and Eliza was known to help numerous people find jobs in the area. (Courtesy of HL.)

Keeping the 1,400 acres at Beauty Ranch intact took all the skill and vigor Eliza could muster. Her son, Irving, began to help her direct the agricultural work as she managed contracts and agreements of copyright. Some of London's works were published posthumously, including *Hearts of Three* and *The Assassination Bureau*, but his fame and the London earning power began to fade, putting the ranch in further jeopardy. (Courtesy of HL.)

Pictured here in 1916, Irving Shepard attended UC Davis and played on the football team. When Jack London died, Irving left college and returned to the ranch to help his mother, Eliza, oversee the livestock. In the coming decade, the House of Happy Walls was built, albeit slowly due to a shortage of funds. Charmian spent much of her time in New York, Hawaii, and Europe. (Courtesy of SF.)

Irving Shepard served in the Navy in World War I and is pictured here with his mother, Eliza. Letters from Irving to Eliza and Charmian show that the ranch and the well-being of his family were much on his mind while he was away. Upon his return, he began in earnest to seek ways to make the ranch solvent. Everyone in the family agreed that keeping Beauty Ranch intact was key. (Courtesy of SF.)

Betrothed

W. Irving Shepard   **Mildred M. Ranker**

Mildred Ranker and Irving Shepard attended high school together and married in 1920. They had four children—Jack, Jill, Milo, and Joy. Both Mildred and Eliza were said to have psychic visions from time to time, and they had a close relationship. Charmian gave Wake Robin Lodge to Eliza as an Easter gift, and Mildred and Irving moved into Eliza's shingled house near the cottage. (Courtesy of SF.)

This photograph, taken in Glen Ellen, shows the lighthearted and warm friendship between Mildred (left) and Eliza. Charmian, Eliza, and Mildred all had unique personalities and enjoyed and supported one another during the early 20th century. Times were changing. The flu epidemic, World War I, Prohibition, women's suffrage, and the Great Depression affected millions and millions of Americans, and these historic events impacted Beauty Ranch. More-rural areas such as Glen Ellen and Beauty Ranch became a welcome respite, and many of the ranch workers were men without resources who came looking for a meal and stayed on to cut wood and tend the livestock. (Courtesy of PN.)

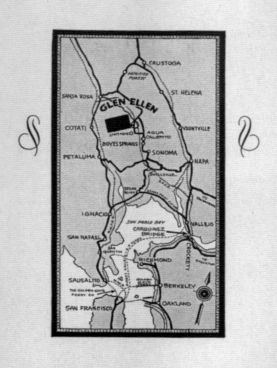

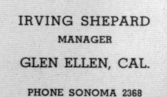

JACK LONDON RANCH

IN THE VALLEY OF THE MOON

In order to survive the economic pressures of the Great Depression, Eliza and Irving began to use the cottage, the old winery, cabins, and other buildings as a guest ranch. Some remodeling was required to prepare for additional guests, and young girls were recruited to help serve meals, clean, and work with the horses. This operation continued from 1935 until around 1948. This promotional brochure describes the riding trails, fresh milk, eggs, and butter, the rustic but charming accommodations, and the incredible views from the mountain. The lake was stocked with fish, and in the summer months boating, swimming, and fly-fishing were a big attraction. (Courtesy of HL.)

Shown here in 1934, the spacious sunporch across the back of the cottage was a gathering place for guests year-round. During the Depression and war years, travel was costly and the proximity of the ranch by train made it an affordable vacation destination for families from San Francisco and Los Angeles. (Courtesy of Sonoma State Library Waring Jones Collection.)

For many decades, Jack London's office remained as it was, with his desks, books, maps, memorabilia, and papers arranged very much as he had them in 1916. Guests could view the room, but no visitors were permitted to enter unless expressly granted access. (Courtesy of Sonoma State University Library.)

At Jack London Ranch

When the guest ranch was opened, the cottage (above) was remodeled, and an enclosed porch and large fireplace were added across from the bunkhouse (below). Guests could take the sun in the courtyard between the two buildings or enjoy a cozy sunporch and fireplace for chilly days and evenings. The bunkhouse was actually the top story of the old winery building and at that time featured small rustic bedrooms, which families and individuals returned to year after year. During World War II, numerous Dutch refugees rescued by submarine from Java were brought to the ranch by Lt. Comdr. Max Viteland of the Royal Dutch Navy to spend time recovering from their harrowing ordeal. (Above, courtesy of Sonoma State University Library; below, courtesy of SH.)

Movie rights were sold for some of London's stories and novels, but both Charmian and Eliza were disappointed in the adaptations, as they were not faithful to the spirit of London's work. Pictured here is the movie placard for 1935 film *The Call of the Wild*, which stars Clark Gable and Loretta Young. (Courtesy of Sonoma State Library Waring Jones Collection.)

Many families returned annually. Pictured on horseback are Charmian London (left) and Isabel Hume, a good friend from Los Angeles. Vacationing at the ranch was a summer ritual for Isabel and her son Stewart, who looked forward to coming to the mountain and experiencing the rustic, charming life in Glen Ellen. (Courtesy of SH.)

Learning horsemanship and other outdoor skills was a great feature at the ranch, and Stewart Hume, pictured here on Smokey, thrived in the natural environment. Stewart is now a valued docent at Jack London State Park and leads tours of the cottage, the very cottage where he had breakfast and dinner 60 years ago. (Courtesy of SH.)

Milo Shepard, Irving's son, was born in 1925. Living on Sonoma Mountain was indeed rural, but cultural excursions, according to Milo, "were the norm. Our class went to the San Francisco Opera, the Symphony, things like that." Nonetheless, Milo found time for his pet fawn, shown here. There were famous visitors to the ranch such as Charles Lindbergh, Cordell Hull, and Ernie Pyle during the Guest Ranch years. (Courtesy of SF.)

Irrigation from the lake was controlled through a valve to water the fields below. Irving Shepard (left) and his son Milo kept the lake from silting in by bulldozing the sediment back toward the mountain in the dry season. By clearing sediment, the lake was kept cool and deep. Natural springs beneath the lakebed and water piped from Graham Creek helped refresh the lake during the summer. (Courtesy of SF.)

Guest Ranch visitors on horseback pictured here are, from left to right, Barbara Landis, Sue Rattry (who later married Milo Shepard), Stewart Hume, Betty Landis, and Romana Von Hofmannsthal, daughter of Ava Astor and granddaughter of Hugo Von Hofmannsthal, famous librettist for Richard Strauss and a cofounder of the Salzburg Festival. (Courtesy of SH.)

In the 1940s, the lake was a refreshing destination, and hikers and horseback riders often took picnics there. The shoulder of Sonoma Mountain sheltered the wind, and all around was silent but for the birdsong. Birthday and Independence Day parties were annual events where neighbors and guests celebrated with barbecue and cake in the sun and under the stars. (Courtesy of SH.)

Stewart Hume is pictured here paddling the long canoe in the lake around 1945. Stewart recalls Ernie Smith, an Olympic swimmer, teaching kids swimming strokes when he visited the ranch with his granddaughter Mickey. Mickey, who now lives on an adjacent ranch, continues to ride horses on Sonoma Mountain today. (Courtesy of SH.)

The Wappo called their chief the headman, and Irving Shepard was often referred to as either "Shep" or "Headman." He was a diligent and focused manager, and as his mother's health began to fail, he stepped in and took on more of the copyright and literary estate management, working with Charmian and Eliza to keep the ranch intact. (Courtesy of SH.)

Throughout the three decades following Jack London's death, efforts were made to secure and sell movie rights to all of London's works. This endeavor met with disappointing results. Often, the script of the movie did not follow the book, or the distribution and sale did not reap the profits expected. Irving and Charmian made trips to Hollywood and New York to negotiate on behalf of the London estate. (Courtesy of SF.)

In 1941, Edward G. Robinson, Ida Lupino, and John Garfield starred in the Warner Bros. rendition of *The Sea Wolf*. The film was popular and gritty, but again, the studio changed the story line. Though these films were shown nationally, Charmian and the Shepard family did not reap great revenue. (Courtesy of Sonoma State University Library.)

Around 1938 at the ranch, Eliza (third from right, with unidentified women) shared the harvest by allowing gleaning. Neighbors could collect fruit once the main harvest was done, without paying, as the orchard benefitted from the late picking. Years after her death, neighbors continued to praise her generous, kind, and practical nature. (Courtesy of HL.)

Eliza Shepard was elected national president of the Women's Auxiliary to the American Legion in 1926 and lived for a year in Washington, DC, where she also participated in the Women's Labor Congress. In 1928, she was a major participant at an international peace conference. While in Washington, she dated Cordell Hull, secretary of state and winner of the Nobel Peace Prize. (Courtesy of SF.)

Eliza Shepard's commitment to veterans' rights and the welfare of women and children continued throughout her life. In 1927, she traveled to London and Paris as national president of the Women's Auxiliary. Letters to Charmian during this trip reveal that Eliza had a wonderful time despite ongoing concerns about ranch business. Irving managed affairs while she was away. (Courtesy of SF.)

When Eliza died in 1939, she was heralded as a distinguished, patriotic woman with a merry laugh and a generous heart. Newspapers across the country acknowledged her contribution to veterans' rights. Hundreds attended her funeral in Sonoma in 1939, and her ashes were placed near Jack London's on Sonoma Mountain. (Courtesy of SF.)

Irving and Mildred lived at the ranch throughout their marriage. All four Shepard children graduated from college, and Jack Shepard and Milo Shepard married and continued to live on the ranch. In 1965, Jack was in a Jeep accident on the mountain and died due to his injuries. Around this time, Milo took a job with California State Parks as a ranger. The dairy operation they had managed was sold off. (Courtesy of SF.)

Throughout her widowhood, Charmian London (pictured) remained vivacious and fashionable. Her efforts to support London's literary and ranch legacies spanned nearly four decades. Milo Shepard recalled Charmian this way: "She worked every day of her life. She was very proud of her abilities. We used to ride by the hour when I was a boy . . . She was very strong, athletic . . . she'd walk in a room and people turned. She was a goer. But she was never in competition with men. She was a beautiful woman into her eighties. She had this aura." Charmian died in 1955, and Beauty Ranch and the London literary trust were willed to Irving Shepard and his descendants. (Courtesy of SH.)

Irving Shepard (left) kept Beauty Ranch together. Irving's four children matured; Jack and Milo served in World War II, and afterward, Jack attended Harvard and Milo graduated from Cal Poly. In the late 1960s, they began a dairy operation, and the brothers married twin sisters, Sue and Marianne Rattry. Milo (below) lived at the ranch full-time. In 1959, Irving deeded 39 acres including the Wolf House ruins, House of Happy Walls, and the gravesite to the State of California. Jack London State Historic Park attracted thousands in the first week. When Jack Shepard died, Milo sold off the dairy cows and became a ranger at Sugarloaf State Park until 1972. As Irving grew older, Milo took on many of the ranch and literary responsibilities. Milo had three children—Neil, Brian, and Lisa—and Neil still lives at the ranch with other Shepard descendants. (Both, courtesy of SF.)

In the early 1970s, Milo Shepard began cultivating grapes on the terraces of Beauty Ranch. The deep soil in this section of the ranch contained minerals and nutrients suited to cabernet. Using a gunsight, Milo laid out the fields and eventually developed 125 acres of high-quality vineyard. Milo's methods are respected and continued by vintners in the valley today. (Courtesy of CS.)

This wine label is from the early days of winemaking. Eventually, all grapes went to Kenwood Winery, where the Jack London Ranch wines would be created and bottled in an exclusive arrangement that has lasted decades. The Shepard grapes have produced medal-winning cabernet, zinfandel, and merlot wines for many decades. (Courtesy of SF.)

The leading London scholars pictured here in 1985 are, from left to right, Russ Kingman, Dr. Earle Labor, and Milo Shepard. Milo and Dr. Labor, along with Robert C. Leitz III, edited a comprehensive three-volume edition of London's correspondence with extensive indexing used by researchers worldwide, *The Letters of Jack London*, published by Stanford University Press in 1988. Shepard, Leitz, and Labor also collaborated on the *Complete Short Stories of Jack London*. Kingman published *A Pictorial Biography of Jack London*, a unique biography featuring many rarely seen images of London and his life. Kingman and his wife, Winnie, operated the Jack London Bookstore in Glen Ellen for many years. In 2012, Dr. Labor published *Jack London, An American Life*, an award-winning biography. (Courtesy of SF.)

Four

Beauty Ranch Becomes a State Park

In 1959, the Irving Shepard Trust granted 39 acres of Beauty Ranch to California State Parks. This gift included the Wolf House Ruins, gravesite, and House of Happy Walls, which serves as a house museum and visitors' center. In the first few days, over 5,000 visitors came from near and far. Today, more than 90,000 visitors come to the expanded park during daylight hours each year. (Courtesy of DL.)

The beautiful craftsmanship of the House of Happy Walls is a testament to the devotion of Charmian London. In the month following her husband's death, she pleaded with the public to keep London's dream alive: "Have any of you thought what is to become of the great thing he has started up here? Have any of you wondered what it would mean to me, who understood, to let his long dream of the land here, lapse, for want of the means to carry it on? . . . I am begging you now, with all my heart, not to let the world forget that he laid his hand upon the hills of California with the biggest writing of all his writing and imagination and wisdom . . . Just don't let all who listen and read and run, forget Jack London's biggest dream." (Courtesy of AS.)

The plaque reads, "This is the 'House of Happy Walls,' built in 1919 by Charmian K. London in memory of her husband, Jack London, renowned author. Here are housed many of his works and the collection gathered in their travels throughout the world. Charmian's house, the ruins of Jack's 'Wolf House,' and his grave were presented in 1960 to the State of California by his nephew, Irving Shepard." (Courtesy of AS.)

The interior of the House of Happy Walls includes reading and sleeping nooks such as the one pictured here. The iron windows, natural wood panels, and gently curved ceilings are evocative of details of the Wolf House. Throughout the building, unique artifacts from the voyage of the *Snark* and Hawaiian travels lend character and delight. (Courtesy of AS.)

The tall, carved wooden dancing sticks on display here are from the Solomon Islands. The shells, attached to leather thongs (pictured at the lower center of the photograph), made signaling sounds acting as a "South Seas wireless." Numerous fertility carvings such as the one featured on the right were incorporated into the design of the building. (Courtesy of AS.)

On the first floor, much of London's library and his desks, typewriters, and papers were arranged to approximate his den. The cottage, where he actually did live and write, was still part of the Shepard family trust so displaying London's office in the park museum was a good way to engage the public. Translated works from around the world are still displayed on the second floor of the House of Happy Walls. (Courtesy of AS.)

84

The estate of Charmian London included an exquisite collection of custom-made gowns and riding apparel. Charmian was ever fashionable and collected handwork from all over the world, which Eliza and seamstresses used to augment Charmian's wardrobe. California State Parks displays a variety of Charmian's clothes and shoes upstairs in the House of Happy Walls. (Courtesy of AS.)

A trail leads from the House of Happy Walls through oak and madrone woodlands to the Wolf House ruins, crossing a small creek and circumnavigating the family orchard and garden plots that London terraced in 1912. Visitors can also trek up a small knoll to view London's gravesite from this same trail. (Courtesy of AS.)

Stark and dark, the ruin stands three stories tall, surrounded by new-growth redwoods 100 years old. Park visitors in 1960 could explore within the ruins but now must remain outside the barriers. Not much has changed within the ruins over the 100-plus years since fire destroyed the Wolf House in 1913. Views from the structure are now obscured by this new tree growth. (Courtesy of AS.)

DEDICATION

NATIONAL HISTORIC LANDMARK

JACK LONDON STATE HISTORIC PARK

GLEN ELLEN , SONOMA COUNTY , CALIF.

MAY 16 , 1964. 1:30 P. M.

In 1964, Jack London State Historic Park was dedicated as a National Historic Landmark, and the ruins, gravesite, and House of Happy Walls were honored with this designation, which protects the structures and the land surrounding them. A ceremony was held at the park to commemorate this important distinction. (Courtesy of HL.)

In 1977 and 1979, the state purchased an additional 756 acres of the Jack London Ranch from the Shepard family, including the working center of London's ranch and buildings such as the cottage, the Pig Palace, barns, and silos. This part of the ranch, shown here from the slope of Sonoma Mountain, has been open since 1979. The winery ruins in the foreground and the cottage, barns, and a glimpse of the House of Happy Walls roof (upper left corner) comprise the heart of Beauty Ranch and the Guest Ranch operated by the Shepard family from 1934 to 1948. The Shepard family retained 160 acres, and Milo Shepard and Irving Shepard began cultivating vines in this fertile section of the ranch. (Courtesy of DL.)

Visitors approach Beauty Ranch along a wide path lined with eucalyptus saplings, where group meeting areas with picnic tables, barbecues, and water are arranged in the shade beneath the forest canopy. Rustic weddings, family picnics, and special small gatherings take place here near the upper parking lot. (Courtesy of AS.)

This 2010 images shows the stone sherry barn (left) built in 1885 and the manure pit and stallion barn built by London's workers in 1912. In this meadow in the park, plays, Plowing Play Day, and picnic gatherings take place today. The cactus exhibit in the foreground commemorates London and Burbank's collaboration to experiment with renewable cattle feed around 1912. (Courtesy of AS.)

Kohler and Frohling winery buildings, purchased by London in 1910, included this distillery (above) and winery ruins (below). For decades, visitors were barred from entry to the distillery due to hazardous conditions. The winery ruins are stone walls that remained after the collapse of the actual winery building during the 1906 earthquake, and a second portion of the winery ruins includes the bunkhouse, pictured in London's time on page 68. Eliza's office and numerous small guest cubicles were part of the wood-frame second story that is no longer present, as it was destroyed by fire in the 1960s while still owned by the Shepard family. (Both, courtesy of AS.)

Throughout the seasons, the vineyard vista in the center of Beauty Ranch brings color and vitality to the park. Trails lead past the vineyard, and a small road allows access to the families living on the 160-acre Shepard Ranch in the center of the park. Red wines produced by Kenwood Winery using grapes from the Shepard Ranch have won prestigious awards for many decades. (Courtesy of CS.)

On a small knoll under a giant oak, the cottage pictured here was originally constructed around 1862 and remodeled and updated through the years. In images earlier in this book, a stone chimney and wide sunporch are present; however, now the cottage porch is narrow and leads to the stone dining room. (Courtesy of AS.)

Facing the garden, the glassed-in porches were sleeping and sunporches for Jack (left) and Charmian (right). The restoration of the cottage began in the late 1980s and sought to duplicate the existing sense of the cottage during London's period from 1910 to 1916. (Courtesy of CS.)

Structural repairs and upgrades were required to house the priceless artifacts to be exhibited within the cottage and stone dining room. Greg Hayes (left), supervising ranger for Jack London State Historic Park, and Lou Leal, historian for VMNHA, were deeply involved in cottage restoration efforts. During the lengthy restoration, a comprehensive photographic display curated by Leal explained the London legacy to visitors. (Courtesy of VMNHA.)

California State Parks and the California State Park Foundation won the prestigious Governor's Award for Historic Preservation for the cottage house museum in 2003. However, state park funds were dwindling, and visitors were only permitted in the cottage one or two days per week due to state park staffing issues. The cottage visitor entrance exhibit is pictured here. (Courtesy of VMNHA.)

In Jack's office, many works of art and first editions were displayed in the two rooms housing his desks, typewriters, many of his papers and books, and interesting items such as a Dictaphone from the period. The writing den was expanded after the Wolf House fire in 1913 and is sheltered by a giant oak said to be over 300 years old. (Courtesy of AS.)

Above Jack London's sleeping cot in the rear of the cottage, visitors can see notes in London's handwriting strung up on clothesline with wooden clothespins. When inspired during the night, London would scrawl notes to himself, Eliza, or Charmian and pin them overhead to be retrieved the next day. (Courtesy of Richard Snyder.)

A lovely restored bedroom, dressing room, and bath displays some of Charmian and Jack's clothing in an armoire faithful to the day, but this formal bedroom was generally used for naps by the couple, who preferred to sleep separately due to Charmian's insomnia and London's late-night habits. (Courtesy of AS.)

Charmian was photographed in her sleeping porch in 1919 (see page 59), and using images from the period, the historical specialists at California State Parks were able to successfully recreate the bohemian, rustic, yet sumptuous feeling of this room. Outside the windows, the gardens during London's time were casual and relaxed and featured some of the couples' favorite flowers. (Courtesy of AS.)

The stone dining room shown here displays many artifacts from numerous travels, including to Korea, Samoa, Fiji, and Hawaii, as well as artwork by London's contemporaries. The gramophone in the room actually made the voyage on the *Snark* and fascinated the natives in the South Seas. Many consider the cottage and stone dining room the heart of Beauty Ranch. (Courtesy of AS.)

The ancient oak beside the cottage is currently being monitored and may be dying. In 2013, acorns from the oak were germinated, and young oaks will be planted in the same location if the tree must be removed. Ceremonies featuring Native American speakers and rituals as well as cultural events have celebrated the life of the tree—believed to be more than 300 years old. (Courtesy of AS.)

Originally, the state intended to create a working farm where visitors could see early 20th-century farming practices, perhaps including pigs in the Pig Palace, pictured here. This piggery is a short hike from the cottage and winery ruins. In 1999, the Pig Palace was restored through funds and labor provided by Benziger Family Winery. See page 51 for a photograph of the Pig Palace shortly after construction. (Courtesy of CS.)

Hidden downhill from the Pig Palace under shelter of oaks, the smokehouse, pictured here, is reached via a short trail created by workers from Benziger Family Winery. This small stone building was present in London's time and has not been used for many years. (Courtesy of Richard Snyder.)

The twin silos rise high in the sky and mystify some visitors. With concrete blocks formed on the site, the silos were completed around 1914, and the roofs were replaced in 1998. When the silos were in use, a conveyor belt with a gasoline engine (rumored to be the only one used by London at his ranch) transported silage to the top. Workers retrieved silage as needed from the bottom. (Courtesy of Richard Snyder.)

Jack London Lake, half a mile up the mountain, officially became part of the park around 1979. The maintenance practices of Milo Shepard were abandoned, and the lake began to silt in, which created a habitat for invasive plants. The siltation and overgrowth of vegetation compromised the natural springs and raised the temperature of the water. Oxygen levels began to drop, and fish, frogs, salamanders, and turtles began to struggle. (Courtesy of VMNHA.)

The log bathhouse constructed to Eliza Shepard's specifications in 1914 remains strong and stable after 100 years. This structure is not open to the public, but visitors can peek in and see changing and showering spaces for men and women separated by curtains. Fresh water was piped in from a natural spring on the mountain, and there was once a stone barbecue and fireplace nearby that has been removed. (Courtesy of Richard Snyder.)

Valley of the Moon Natural History Association (VMNHA) was formed in 1982 to support state parks with visitor education and publications in three state parks. Over the years, many important efforts have been led by VMNHA. Jack London Lake Alliance, formed by the author of this book in 2008, sponsored efforts to fully restore the lake. At a fundraising event, she holds a placard showing Irving Shepard fishing in the clean, clear lake. (Courtesy of CS.)

Funds raised by the Lake Alliance paid for reports, surveys, engineering studies, and special requirements, such as the red-legged frog survey. The man appearing half buried in a pasture is actually in the lake, which, beginning in 2010, became completely choked with algae. Over $400,000 has been spent by the state and the Lake Alliance, yet no actual cleanup has begun. (Courtesy of Richard Snyder.)

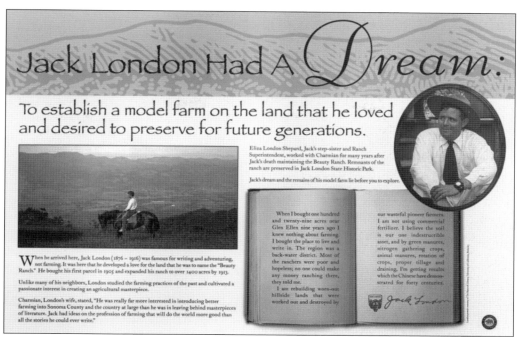

The large panels are placed at points of interest throughout the park. This panel greets visitors as they crest the small hill leading into Beauty Ranch from the upper parking lot. Note the historical feeling and the references to London's literary as well as his farming legacies. The addition of the panels helps inform more than 90,000 visitors annually. (Courtesy of David Price.)

The evocative and informative panels installed throughout the park are the result of a successful collaboration between VMNHA and state parks. In 2008, panels designed by David Price using research provided by VMNHA and park staff were installed in numerous locations. Sheryl Lawton, park ranger (far right), directs state employees and retired ranger Greg Hayes (second from left), who became board president of VMNHA. (Courtesy of Richard Snyder.)

VMNHA began training docents in 1988 for three state parks—Annadel, Sugarloaf, and Jack London State Historic Park. Here, VMNHA president Greg Hayes (center) answers trainees questions about the Wolf House fire. In 2010, Matt Atkinson and Greg Hayes, both former park rangers and VMNHA board members, published a book about the building and the loss of the Wolf House. This book is sold online and in the bookstores at the park. (Courtesy of VMNHA.)

In 2008, the anniversary of Beauty Ranch as a state park was commemorated through events funded and hosted by VMNHA. The Celebrate the Park event in the winery ruins featured creations from local chefs, a photography exhibit, special tours of the cottage, and music by the Sonoma Town Band as well as jazz from the Jim Castrone Trio (pictured in foreground). (Courtesy of CS.)

A fundraising dinner, Moonlight Adventure at Jack's (pictured), was hosted by VMNHA to raise funds for costs no longer covered through state park funds. Mounting concerns about repairs, improvements, and natural resource management were reported in all state parks, and Jack London Park felt the pinch as funds dwindled for more than a decade. (Courtesy of CS.)

The Piano Club at the park was formed by Jud Goodrich (pictured playing Charmian's concert grand Steinway given to her by Jack, intended for the Wolf House). The Piano Club volunteers perform for several hours each weekend day in the House of Happy Walls. Beginning in 2010, the club decided to host special concerts for fundraising and have successfully raised thousands of dollars for the park. (Courtesy of VMNHA.)

The upstairs sitting room of the House of Happy Walls is just large enough to provide seating for an intimate crowd for concerts, usually performed around Mother's Day, Valentine's Day, and sometimes in the fall. Here, the crowd is preparing for one of six performers to fill the building with beautiful music. Park visitors love to hear the music resonating inside and cascading through the windows to the oak woodlands beyond. (Courtesy of VMNHA.)

When the cottage was restored, the exhibit of Jack London's office, formerly housed in the House of Happy Walls, was moved to the cottage where he lived, wrote, and died. VMNHA historians and docents, with the help of designer David Price, created an exhibit capturing the incredible voyage of the *Snark*. This image shows just one portion of the captivating exhibit. (Courtesy of David Price).

In 2002, the state annexed 600 acres adjoining the park, increasing the total size of the park to 1,400 acres, though not the exact same 1,400 acres London owned originally. The old orchard pictured here is part of the new addition to the park. Heritage varieties of apples, pears, prunes, and apricots over 100 years old continue to bear fruit. (Courtesy of DL.)

Many acres of trees were originally planted as part of the Sonoma Home for the Feeble Minded, later renamed the Sonoma Development Center. The orchards, in addition to a dairy, pig farm, chicken houses, cannery, and vegetable gardens supplied the center residents and staff in Glen Ellen. Provender produced in quantity was traded with similar operations run by the state in the Central Valley. (Courtesy of DL.)

Along with the orchard addition, the park annexed a unique feature, a 2,000-year-old redwood tree, often referred to as the Grandmother Tree or the Ancient Redwood. Pictured here is a portion of the tree showing the strange formation of a kind of candelabra effect whereby the tree grew to the side rather than vertically. This feature may have prevented it from being felled when surrounding trees were clear-cut on the mountain between 1890 and 1908. Although the coast redwood is the tallest living thing in the world, this particular tree may have lost its top to a fire, therefore it does not tower over the forest canopy and make its presence known. When the rest of the old-growth forest was logged, this tree was spared. (Courtesy of DL.)

When the additional acreage was brought in, new trails were opened up, and old roads were decommissioned by state park staff. By 2012, nearly 28 miles of hiking, biking, and horseback trails were accessible through Jack London State Historic Park. Maintaining these trails and roads was costly, and volunteers from VMNHA and Sonoma County Trails Council pitched in. Mountain Trail is pictured here in 2012. (Courtesy of DL.)

Hikers can summit Sonoma Mountain and also hike on portions of the Bay Area Ridge Trail. Vistas from the mountain include Mount Diablo, San Pablo Bay, San Francisco Bay, and the Mayacamas Range. Most of the trails are partially shady, and rare wildflowers and mushrooms are sighted when in season. (Courtesy of DL.)

From the Ridge Trail, this vista of the Valley of the Moon today seems to correspond very closely with the image shown on page 11. Vineyards in the valley have replaced other crops, and the logging and development resulted in some change, but for the most part the scene remains very close to how it appeared 100 years ago. (Courtesy of DL.)

In 2011, budget issues slated 72 California state parks for closure. A legislative order, authored by then congressman Jared Huffman (center), allowed nonprofits to secure contracts to operate individual parks. In 2012, VMNHA became the first nonprofit to win a state contract. The author and Greg Hayes are pictured here at the state capitol presenting VMNHA's proposal to Congressman Huffman. (Courtesy of VMNHA.)

Five

SAVING BEAUTY RANCH

In 2012, VMNHA began operating the park, and the new staff and board partnered with key community groups to boost efficiency and revenue. From left to right are Stephan Stubbins, Brad Surosky (Transcendence Theatre Company [TTC]), Betsy Kutska (VMNHA treasurer), Amy Miller (TTC), Chuck Levine (VMNHA president), and Tjiska Van Wyk (executive director of VMNHA), who used entrepreneurial models to leverage the appeal of London and the outdoors. (Courtesy of Ray Mabry.)

Transcendence Theatre Company mounts four shows with 14 or more performances at the park every summer. TTC's Broadway Under the Stars attracts over 10,000 attendees annually from five surrounding counties to its award-winning shows and provides much-needed revenue to the park. Guests picnic in the nearby meadow with food and beverages provided by local food trucks and wineries. (Courtesy of Melania Mahoney.)

Local theater supporters open their homes each summer to 50 or more TTC performers and support crew who fly in from New York, Las Vegas, Los Angeles, and San Francisco for two weeks or more. The informal gatherings before the show in the meadow at Beauty Ranch are fun for locals and first-time visitors alike. (Courtesy of Melania Mahoney.)

The energy generated by the young performers trained at the TTC summer program at the park is a tremendous boost, and hearing their songs ring out while they rehearse is fun for everyone hiking by. The evening shows where the children perform are called Fantastical Family Night, and performances sell out each summer. (Courtesy of Marjorie LeWitt.)

Artistic director Amy Miller is joined onstage with principals from TTC during an end-of-season gala show in the old winery ruins in 2014. The stone walls make a resonant and earthy backdrop for the vibrant and visionary work of the company. Each year, the themes tie in with London's legacy. (Courtesy of Candy Glass Productions.)

As night falls, the performance takes on a dramatic energy. The giant oak near the cottage is lit from below, and music, applause, and laughter ring out within the walls of the old winery ruins, bringing vitality and joy to Beauty Ranch in the Valley of the Moon. An average of 700 people attended each performance in 2014, many who had never before been to the park. (Courtesy of Ryan Daffern.)

To preserve the health of the aged oak and prevent damage to the nearby historic cottage, some branches were trimmed in 2013. As mentioned in chapter 4, seedlings of this oak will be transplanted when the oak no longer thrives. State park specialists continue to monitor natural resources at the park. (Courtesy of AS.)

The park offers many new classes and events to inspire and delight visitors of all ages. Shown here is a watercolor class, the first to be hosted at the park in over 50 years. The staff and nearly 400 volunteers bring a spirit of hospitality that is both welcoming to visitors and receptive to new ideas, helping create relevant and meaningful new park programs. (Courtesy of DL.)

Birding for Children is another fascinating outing designed to inspire young people to get outdoors for experiential activities that increase their appreciation of nature. Sonoma Birding, a local nonprofit, instituted the Christmas Bird Count (now a national event) here in Sonoma Valley. Children and parents are eager to learn about the migrating and native birds flitting through the area. (Courtesy of DL.)

Earth Day clean up is an annual event at the park, and volunteers from REI, California State Parks Foundation, CamelBak, Benziger Winery, and Bay Area Ridge Trail, as well as park docents participate in alternate years. Trail work and park cleanup is an everyday task, but having help from the neighboring businesses and nonprofits is a real boost. (Courtesy of Richard Snyder.)

The Jack London Book Club began in 2013 with the intention of focusing on London's work and inviting readers to explore themes in a collegial setting. Susan Nuernberg (left) and Iris Dunkel are well-known London scholars and published writers who lead the book studies at the park. Jack London continues to intrigue readers, and studying his work in his own backyard is very special. (Courtesy of DL.)

Speaking of volunteers, pictured here is Stewart Hume, who is shown as a young boy in chapter 3. Hume leads guided tours of the cottage on weekends and is one of more than 400 volunteers active in the park today. Docents with interests in history, nature, art, literature, and hiking find meaningful opportunities to lead tours and interpretive activities at Beauty Ranch. The cottage is now open every day. (Courtesy of Richard Snyder.)

The lovely garden beside the cottage has a small pond stocked with koi. Here, a school group explores the garden and the pond in 2014 as part of a day trip arranged through the park's school curriculum tour program. Children are fascinated by London's writing, and introducing them to early 20th-century life is a delight; so much has changed in the past 100 years beyond the boundaries of the ranch. (Courtesy of DL.)

Dominic and Erin Ellis own and operate Triple Creek Horse Outfit and provide guided rides through the park and up the mountain. They are both devoted to the legacy of Jack London and include tales of the trails' history as they guide riders. In 2012, they returned to the park through an agreement with JLPP and provide horseback riding tours year-round. After a horseback ride, one is given a pass for a cottage tour at the park as well as tickets for complimentary tastings at neighboring Benziger Family Winery and nearby Imagery Estate Winery. (Courtesy of Julie Vader.)

For many park visitors, the best way to reach the backcountry is astride, and more than a few interesting things have happened in the backcountry on the rides, including a number of surprise marriage proposals. The gentle horses and expert guides bring back a bit of history to the ranch, and JLPP and park visitors are very happy to see Triple Creek back on the trails. Erin Ellis is pictured here leading riders along Mountain Trail to the lake. (Courtesy of Julie Vader.)

Visitors appreciate the matching Clydesdale teams that Neil Shepard brings out for special occasions in the park and in the community. Neil, great-grandson of Eliza Shepard, lives at the Shepard Ranch and has a wheelwright business as well as his custom carriage rentals. (Courtesy of Richard Snyder.)

Plow and Play Day events have taken place annually and continue at the park today. Farming techniques, rope making, spinning, and steam engines are demonstrated in the broad meadow below the stone barns. Here, a team is being used in the same manner that farmers harrowed over 100 years ago. (Courtesy of CS.)

When JLPP took over operation, many trails were in poor condition. Pictured here is the lovely Cowan Meadow Trail, which was completely overgrown and had given way in one low area. Maintaining and improving trails requires dedicated operations staff and many volunteers. JLPP is proud of the trail improvements throughout the park, including improved signage. (Courtesy of DL.)

On misty days, the Mountain Trail pictured here is like a dreamland. Much of the trail is under leafy canopy, so even in light rain it is a happy hike to the summit. The adventurous hiker can continue past the summit along the ridge on the North Slope Trail and log 18 miles round-trip or take the ridge to the East Slope loop, descend to the orchard via Coon Trap, and return home on Fallen Bridge for a 13-mile loop. (Courtesy of DL.)

Rest areas are arranged along some trails in areas of shade or vistas. From this bench on Mountain Trail, much of the Valley of the Moon can be viewed. There are picnic tables in Beauty Ranch beside and below the cottage, at the Wolf House, and in the group picnic area. On the mountain and near the Ancient Redwood, picnic tables and horse tie-ups are available in the shade. (Courtesy of DL.)

The Mounted Assistance Unit (MAU) has been active in the park for decades. Current president Dr. Jo Dean Nicolette and JLPP president Chuck Levine are among the many patrollers visitors encounter in the backcountry. MAU provides bike and horse patrol services within the park and is available to assist in locating lost hikers, giving directions, answering questions, and providing historical information about London and the land. They are often the first to identify and report hazards on trails and assist in their removal. In several instances, they have been the first responders to hikers requiring assistance. Nearly 100 MAU volunteers contribute 6,000 to 7,000 hours of volunteer service annually at three state parks in the Sonoma Valley, including Jack London State Historic Park. (Courtesy of Richard Snyder.)

Every year, the Benziger Family Winery employees spend time clearing trails, improving structures, or laying gravel. This community service on Earth Day 2008 makes the park safer by reducing fire danger and smoothing trails for hikers. Benziger Family Winery is located on London Ranch Road, and the cooperative relationship between neighbors is deeply valued. (Courtesy of Richard Snyder.)

Park visitors treasure the changing seasons, especially as seen in the vineyard with Sonoma Mountain in the background. Sharing this land as a public park is a gift the Shepard family made possible through their arrangements with the state decades ago. Since then, millions of visitors from throughout the world have experienced what London prized and wrote about so many years ago. (Courtesy of DL.)

Mountain Trail skirts the vineyards and leads to the Lower Lake Trail, a narrow and intimate "hikers only" trail that allows visitors to immerse themselves in nature. The tall redwoods, soft footing, birdsong, and breeze bring a storybook feeling to the experience. In August, ripe blackberries line the trail, and dappled sun filters down in the silence. For 75 years, the lake was a key resource for irrigation, fishing, boating, and swimming. Charmian and ranch guests rode their horses bareback into the cool water, and herons nested on the far shore. If the lake is restored, visitors could again swim and wade in the cool water, and birds and wildlife would enjoy the wetland preserve to be retained on a portion the former lakebed. (Courtesy of DL.)

The seemingly timeless stone buildings stand sentinel halfway up Sonoma Mountain. Beneath this beauty are challenges that must be faced in the coming years. Stone structures need repair, the unsightly temporary caps on the old winery walls need to be removed, and the lake and dam are in dire need of restoration. JLPP is committed to raising funds through local and national efforts to solve these major deferred maintenance problems. (Courtesy of CS.)

The stone dam and the lake (clogged with sediment and algae) were named one of the most threatened cultural landscapes in America in 2012 by the Cultural Landscape Foundation, a national nonprofit. This once refreshing respite is dying despite the public's desire to save it. Solving the sedimentation in the streams was one of Jack London's original intentions when he created the dam and lake in 1914. By dredging the lake back to original levels, reshaping the slope at the banks, and retaining about half the marshy area as a wetland, the intention and historical appearance can be regained while also creating protected habitat for wood ducks and other birds and wildlife. To see the lake as it once was, see pages 52 and 53. (Courtesy of DL.)

Deep erosion gullies scar the hillside below the dam. This serious erosion increases sediment downstream and affects steam sedimentation levels, which in turn affects fish and wildlife habitats for several miles downstream. Correcting the erosion below the dam (caused by a faulty spillway design installed in the 1980s) is part of the Lake Alliance proposal. (Courtesy of DL.)

May's Meadow, also known as May's Clearing, is an incredible vista where on a cloudless day Mount Diablo, 60 miles away as the crow flies, can be easily seen. Waterways and low mountains ringing the Valley of the Moon can be seen in the distance, and the orchard is visible in the low valley downhill about a mile away. (Courtesy of DL.)

Mountain Trail is open to horses, bicycles, and hikers. When the trail photograph includes a person trekking along, it is possible to understand the incredible scale of the second-growth redwoods present on the mountain. These majestic trees are descendants of the mighty old-growth forest that once sheltered Native Americans and wildlife for thousands of years. (Courtesy of DL.)

On the Fourth of July, the nighttime view from this bench reveals colorful fireworks celebrations in more than 10 towns far in the distance, including Sonoma, Richmond, and Vallejo, and ghostly glows from the twin fireworks shows on the bay in San Francisco. (Courtesy of DL.)

Brilliant maples, flowering buckeye, redwood, madrone, oak, bay, and manzanita trees thrive on the slopes of the mountain. The quiet stillness of the backcountry attracts hikers with a lifelong love of the park. New visitors are thrilled with the great variety of trails, from easy to strenuous, each revealing special magic on the mountain. The 23 miles within the park boundary connect with more than 10 miles of additional wildlife corridor trails open to the public. Organizations like Sonoma Trails Council work hand in hand with the operations manager at the park and local volunteers to keep the trails in good order. (Courtesy of DL.)